THE TESLA YC

KNOW

Unknown Facts, Inventions and Much More about Nikola Tesla

Author: Hollie Kruse

Copyright © 2024 Vancour

All rights reserved.

DEDICATION

Dedicated to our readers.

BOOK CONTENTS

NIKOLA TESLA: THE GENIUS INNOVATOR AHEAD OF HIS TIME — 1

PICTURING, DESIGNING, INVENTING — 6

WHAT TESLA GAVE THE WORLD? — 20

A CLOSER LOOK AT MR. TESLA! — 38

SO MUCH MORE ABOUT TESLA... — 48

THE ONE WHO LIT THE WORLD — 57

NIKOLA TESLA: THE GENIUS INNOVATOR AHEAD OF HIS TIME

You probably do not pay much thought to how something works or to the individuals who made it all possible when you turn on a switch or a lamp. You might say Thomas Alva Edison, the man who created the incandescent light bulb if you were required to identify the genius behind the lamp. Yet, a visionary by the name of Nikola Tesla was equally as influential, if not more so.

One of the greatest inventors and visionaries in history, Nikola Tesla is known for his ingenuity and genius. Tesla, who was born on July 10th, 1856, in Smiljan, Croatia, changed electrical engineering and the way we harness and use energy. The basis for Tesla's extraordinary career was built by his upbringing and schooling. He started working for famed inventor Thomas Edison after completing his engineering and physics school. Yet, their divergent perspectives on the development of electricity resulted in a bitter conflict known as the "War of Currents". From a young age, Tesla showed a remarkable aptitude for science and engineering. He was fascinated by the natural world, and he spent hours experimenting with electrical circuits and other scientific phenomena. He was also a voracious reader, and he devoured books on physics, mathematics, and other scientific subjects. At an early age, Tesla's intelligence and creativity were clear to see. He was able to mentally see intricate systems and procedures, and he could come up with creative answers to issues that seemed impossible to solve. He was a talented artist as well, and his scientific work frequently reflected his aesthetic sensibility.

Tesla's life was not without its difficulties, despite his numerous accomplishments. The scientific and engineering establishment of his time frequently misunderstood and undervalued him, and he struggled to obtain financial support for his research. Additionally, he struggled with mental health issues such as anxiety and depression, making it frequently challenging for him to maintain stable relationships. Tesla used to be a complicated and multifaceted individual, and his character and creativity proceed to encourage new generations of scientists and engineers. He used to be a first-rate inventor and engineer; however, he used to be additionally a deeply compassionate and empathetic individual who used to be dedicated to the use of his skills to make the world a higher place.

Tesla is known for his eccentric personality and unusual habits. He has an exceptional memory and claims to have visualized his inventions vividly before making them. Tesla also was fascinated by pigeons and had a strong connection with them, even claiming to receive important information and inspiration from this bird. Despite his genius, Tesla faced financial difficulties throughout his life and struggled to get the recognition he deserved. He often prioritizes his work over financial gain, leaving some of his projects unfinished and inventions unpatented. However, Tesla's impact on modern society cannot be overstated. His inventions laid the foundations for the electrification of the world and paved the way for many technological advances. Tesla died on January 7, 1943, leaving behind a legacy that continues to inspire scientists, engineers, and inventors. His vision and foresight paved the way for the development of the myriad technologies we rely on today, from the power grid and wireless communications to electric motors and renewable energy systems. As we benefit from the fruits of his labour, it is essential to recognize and appreciate the profound impact Tesla had on shaping the future of electricity and technology.

PICTURING, DESIGNING, INVENTING

The legendary electrical engineering genius and inventor Nikola Tesla had a mind that was beyond the ordinary. Unique creative visualization, a photographic memory, and strong practicality set him apart from his peers and were central to his creative process. A testament to his exceptional cognitive abilities, Tesla was able to picture his inventions with astonishment, meticulously design them, and then bring them to life. Tesla's remarkable ability to visualize was at the heart of his creative process. He could paint intricate and precise images of his inventions on a canvas like his mind did. Tesla would immerse himself in extensive mental exploration before beginning any kind of physical construction. With eyes shut, he would intellectually gather and control the different parts, imagining their exact structure, capability, and interconnections. Tesla's visualisation technique was a vivid and powerful experience rather than merely a form of daydreaming. He could view his creations from a variety of angles and perspectives because of the incredibly precise images that would appear in his mind's eye. He had the ability to mentally hone and perfect plans, confirming their effectiveness and viability before moving forward with the physical execution. Tesla's photographic memory played a crucial role in his exceptional capacity for visualisation. He had a remarkable ability to take in a tremendous quantity of knowledge, from mathematical calculations and scientific theories to mechanical and electrical engineering concepts. Tesla was able to recall and retain a tremendous amount of information with ease because his mind worked like a sizable library. His creative ideas were formed on the foundation of this mental database of knowledge. His own theoretical theories and observations made while doing his tests led him to be sceptical of the commonly accepted model of atomic structure. Tesla disagreed with the conventional scientific wisdom that says that electrons and other tiny subatomic particles make up an atom. He said that the idea of electrons producing an electric charge was incorrect and that electrons, if any existed at all, had no direct connection to electricity. Tesla proposed a fourth state of matter, which he referred to as an "electronic state" or "sub-atom". In contrast to typical atmospheric conditions, he hypothesized that this state of matter could only be observed in an extremely rarefied or experimental vacuum. Tesla held the belief that this sub-atom state was the cause of electrical phenomena and had distinct properties. Nikola Tesla's claims about his very own bodily precept and his alleged improvement of a dynamic idea of gravity have been the difficulty of a whole lot of speculation and debate. While Tesla made statements related to these ideas, it is vital to word that he did now not supply comprehensive written documentation or scientific papers outlining these theories. As a result, the specific nature and validity of Tesla's claims continue to be unclear, and no, addition, proof or elaboration of these theories has been discovered in his writings. Without any supporting evidence or published works by Tesla, it is difficult to evaluate the specifics of his assertions of a physical principle and a dynamic theory of gravity. Although it is possible that Tesla was experimenting with novel concepts and theories concerning matter, energy, and gravity, it is difficult to assess the scientific validity or quality of these statements in the absence of thorough justifications or supporting data.

Tesla's photographic memory enabled him to draw on past experiences, and observations in constructing his mental images. He could easily recall scientific literature, diagrams, and equations and seamlessly integrate them into his mental visualizations. This unique combination of visual memory and encyclopaedic knowledge of Tesla enables the design of complex and technically sound inventions. What distinguished Tesla was his practical intensity in the inventive process. His visualizations were not imaginative; they have been carefully designed with practicality and real-world application in mind. Tesla was aware of the limitations of existing technologies and the practical challenges they would face. Therefore, his mental designs were not mere fantasies, but sophisticated solutions that took into account technical limitations and feasibility. Tesla's practicality was demonstrated in his ability to anticipate potential problems and create innovative solutions within his mental visualizations. He mentally ran simulations and tests, considering various scenarios and refining his designs to mitigate potential flaws or imperfections. This pragmatic approach, combined with his exceptional visualization skills, allowed Tesla to introduce innovative inventions that changed the world. Furthermore, Tesla's images were not limited to single inventions; he could see the interconnectedness of his works within a larger system. He had a unique ability to anticipate the integration of multiple inventions and technologies and how they can work in synergy and create transformative impact.

In his autobiography, Nikola Tesla recounts his extraordinary ability to visualize a specific apparatus and subsequently test-run it in his mind, disassemble it mentally, and evaluate its performance and condition. This remarkable process highlights Tesla's exceptional cognitive skills and his profound understanding of engineering principles. After testing the apparatus mentally, Tesla would proceed to disassemble it in his mind's eye. This involved mentally taking apart the components, examining them, and assessing their wear and tear. Through his incredible visual recall and comprehensive understanding of engineering principles, he could evaluate the condition of each component and determine if any adjustments or replacements were necessary. Tesla's highly developed imagination and excellent spatial awareness allowed him to envisage a complicated device with such clarity and precision. He had a remarkable ability to visualise complex designs and precisely put them together in his mind. He was able to see the device's numerous parts, their placement, and their linkages by imagining it. Tesla would imagine the device being built and then simulate how it would work. This comprised operating the device in a simulated setting, watching how it behaved, and evaluating how well it performed. He was able to spot potential weaknesses, inefficiencies, or areas that needed further work through this mental simulation. The course of intellectually dismantling the mechanical assembly permitted Tesla to acquire bits of knowledge about common sense and the unwavering quality of his plan. He could identify potential weak points or failure-prone areas by evaluating the components' wear and tear. He was guided by this information as he refined the design and made the necessary adjustments to improve the apparatus's overall performance and durability. It is essential to keep in mind that Tesla's exceptional visualization skills were not the only factor in his capacity to mentally test, run, and disassemble an apparatus. His in-depth comprehension of the underlying scientific and engineering principles that governed the apparatus's behaviour also contributed to it. Tesla's broad information and involvement with electrical designing permitted him to precisely re-enact the connections among parts and foresee their usefulness. The accuracy of Tesla's intellectual trying out and disassembling method was regularly proven when he bodily constructed and examined the equipment in reality. More frequently than not, the actual performance was carefully aligned with his intellectual simulations, testifying to the reliability of his visualization abilities. His inventive visualization, coupled with his extensive understanding and realistic experience, allowed him to simulate the behaviour and consider the situation of the apparatus with tremendous accuracy. Tesla's terrific method demonstrates the electricity of the human idea when harnessed to its fullest potential.

As we said earlier, Tesla possessed a photographic memory, a mental faculty that allowed him to retain detailed visual information with remarkable accuracy. This meant that he could memorize intricate blueprints and specifications of his inventions simply by studying them. Once he internalized this information, he no longer needed to refer to physical blueprints or written documents during the manufacturing phase. Having the blueprints and specifications ingrained in his reminiscence furnished Tesla with numerous advantages. Firstly, it allowed him to work with unparalleled efficiency. Without the want to continuously refer to bodily documents, he may want to proceed with the manufacturing method seamlessly, removing time-consuming steps such as retrieving, examining, and decoding blueprints. This streamlined strategy enabled him to work unexpectedly and limit interruptions, for that reason growing productivity. Furthermore, Tesla's potential to work with all the blueprints and specs in his head are more suitable for his adaptability and flexibility for the duration of the manufacturing process. In case changes or changes have been required, he ought to shortly recall the indispensable important points and make the fundamental adjustments besides the want for exterior references. This saved time and allowed for seamless changes to the diagram or manufacturing process, making sure the foremost outcomes. Tesla was able to create things without actual blueprints in part because of his profound mastery of engineering principles. He knew everything there was to know about electrical engineering, mathematics, and physics. He was able to comprehend the fundamental ideas and connections behind his creations thanks to this thorough understanding.

Using this information, Tesla could mentally picture the construction process, foresee difficulties, and make judgments without constantly referring to drawings.

It should be noted that Tesla's ability to work with all the plans and specifications in his head was not limited to just photographic memory. It was the result of his relentless pursuit of knowledge, relentless curiosity, and relentless quest to understand the intricacies of his inventions. Tesla's passion for his work enabled him to internalize complex concepts and visualize them with exceptional clarity. This enabled him to streamline the manufacturing process, work with the remarkable efficiency, and make corrections or changes on the fly.

WHAT TESLA GAVE THE WORLD?

We have heard this genius, Tesla, changed the way we use electricity or energy today. In January 1880, Thomas Edison introduced his electric light bulb to the public, a milestone in the development of electric lighting. This seminal invention provided a practical and efficient alternative to gas lamps and paved the way for the widespread use of electric lighting systems. Shortly after the lamp's introduction, Edison began implementing the new power system in New York's First Circuit. Edison's electrical system was designed to enable the large-scale production, distribution, and use of electricity. It consisted of several key components including generators, transmission lines, and distribution grids. The 1st District of New York served as a testing ground for this innovative system. The installation of Edison's electrical system in the First Ward brought electric lighting to the streets, businesses, and homes of New York. The previously dimly lit streets were now illuminated with the brilliance of electric lamps, enhancing visibility and safety during night-time hours. The installation also allowed businesses and homes to enjoy the convenience and efficiency of electric lighting, replacing the more cumbersome and dangerous gas lighting systems of the day.

Edison's power system was based on direct current (DC), which involved the central generation of electricity in power plants and its distribution to consumers via a cable network. The First Ward of New York City became a showcase for electric power's potential, demonstrating its feasibility and reliability in practical applications. The successful implementation of the system in New York City laid the groundwork for expanding power infrastructure to an additional area, eventually leading to the electrification of entire cities and regions. However, Edison's direct current system had limitations, particularly in terms of transmitting electricity over long distances. This led to the rise of Nikola Tesla's alternating current (AC) system, which offered significant advantages in terms of efficiency and long-distance transmission capabilities.

The "War of Currents", in which AC emerged as the dominant power transmission technology, would eventually take place as a result of the competition between Tesla's AC system and Edison's DC system. Edison's introduction of the electric incandescent lamp and the installation of his power system in the First District of New York City were crucial in popularizing electric lighting and laying the groundwork for the widespread use of electricity in a variety of applications, despite the eventual prevalence of AC power systems. The development of practical electric power systems and Edison's contributions to electrical engineering are still significant junctures in the history of electrification and have had a long-lasting impact on the way our cities are illuminated and powered today.

Nikola Tesla, the notable inventor, and visionary, continually modified the direction of electrical energy transmission with his fresh invention of alternating contemporary (AC). Tesla's AC cutting-edge gadget revolutionized the way electrical energy is generated, transmitted, and utilized, laying the basis for the present-day electrical grid. Prior to Tesla's AC present-day system, the predominant structure of electrical electricity transmission used to be based totally on direct modern (DC). However, DC electricity confronted several limitations, in particular in phrases of its capability to correctly transmit electrical energy over lengthy distances. DC structures suffered from large energy loss and required popular and expensive infrastructure installations to hold voltage levels. Recognizing the shortcomings of DC, Tesla set out to increase a choice that would overcome these challenges. He targeted his efforts on alternating current, a machine that concerned unexpectedly altering the course of the electrical current. Tesla understood that AC had the doable to revolutionize electrical strength transmission due to its capacity to transmit electrical energy effectively over long distances with minimal energy loss.

The invention of the induction motor was one of the most important components of Tesla's AC system. This motor could convert electrical energy into mechanical energy by using AC power to create a rotating magnetic field. Tesla embarked on a series of daring experiments and public demonstrations to demonstrate the potential of AC power. The "War of the Currents", a fierce competition between Tesla's AC system and Thomas Edison's DC system, is one of history's most famous events. The superiority of Tesla's AC system was demonstrated by powering homes, businesses, and even street lighting over long distances.

After the successful implementation of the Niagara Falls hydroelectric power project, Tesla's AC current system gained recognition and widespread acceptance. The practicality and effectiveness of Tesla's invention were demonstrated by harnessing Niagara Falls to generate AC power on a large scale. The project signalled the dawn of a new era in the transmission of electricity and demonstrated the enormous potential of AC power for urban areas. Tesla's discovery of AC current has had an on-going impact. The contemporary electrical grid, which supplies electricity to our buildings, businesses, industries, and modern technology, is mostly dependent on the transmission of AC power. The world's electrification was made possible by Tesla's innovation, which paved the way for the widespread use of electric appliances, lighting systems, motors, and much other electrical equipment.

The ground-breaking work that Tesla did with remote control changed many industries and set the stage for many new developments in automation, communication, and entertainment. Not only did he make the remote control more convenient, but he also opened up a whole new world of possibilities that have since shaped our modern society. Tesla's interest in remote control stemmed from his desire to overcome physical limitations and enable remote device control. His imaginative mind envisioned a world in which machines could be controlled from a distance, freeing humans from the constraints of physical contact. This thought, combined with his profound comprehension of electrical design and remote transmission, moved Tesla to investigate and foster controller innovation. The development of the tele-automation system is one of the significant contributions that Tesla made to the field of remote control. Through the transmission of electrical signals, this system made it possible to control mechanical devices. By remotely controlling a boat, Tesla demonstrated the potential of his tele-automation system to control machinery without direct human intervention. The magnitude of Tesla's invention of faraway manipulation lies in its transformative influence on a few industries. One of the earliest and most exceptional functions used to be in the area of transportation. Tesla's faraway manipulate technological know-how paved the way for the improvement of remote-operated motors and guided systems. Today, far-off manipulation is drastically utilized in the automotive, aerospace, and maritime sectors, enabling safer operations, environment-friendly navigation, and greater precision. Furthermore, far-flung manipulation science has performed a pivotal position in the subject of automation. Tesla's invention laid the basis for the improvement of computerized structures that may want to be managed remotely. This has led to accelerated efficiency, multiplied productivity, and reduced human intervention in a variety of industries, ranging from manufacturing and robotics to agriculture and healthcare. Remote management has converted the way we interact with machines, enabling complicated operations and far-off monitoring in real-time. The impact of Tesla's invention of the remote control is also evident in the field of communications. Remote control technology has been incorporated into various communication devices, such as TVs, radios, and smartphones. This allows users to easily use and navigate through various functions and features, enhancing user experience and convenience. Remote controls have become an integral part of our daily lives, allowing us to interact remotely with a multitude of devices.

In addition to practical applications, the invention of the Tesla remote control also opened up new possibilities in the field of entertainment. Remote control toys, drones, and video game controllers have become popular, providing users with immersive and interactive experiences. The ability to control devices wirelessly has enhanced entertainment options, allowing individuals to enter virtual worlds, experience thrilling adventures, and explore new horizons. The significance of Tesla's invention of the remote control extends beyond tangible applications. It represents a profound shift in the human-machine interface, highlighting the power of technology to transcend physical barriers. Remote control technology has empowered us to manipulate and interact with our surroundings from a distance, fostering convenience, efficiency, and innovation.

Tesla found the concept of wireless energy transmission to be fascinating and thought that it could be accomplished by using high-voltage electrical discharges. In the late 1890s, he started experimenting with different wireless energy transmitter designs. In 1891, he filed a patent for his first invention, a "method of conveying electrical energy without wires".

Tesla coils are the result of years of testing and perfecting Tesla's original design. It consists of a primary coil, connected to the power supply, and a secondary coil, connected to a capacitor. When the primary coil is energized, it generates a high-voltage discharge that is transmitted to the secondary coil, where it is amplified and replayed as a high-frequency electromagnetic wave. Tesla was so impressed with the potential of the Tesla coil that he gave several public demonstrations of its capabilities, including a famous one at the 1893 World's Fair in Chicago, where he lit light 200 bulbs wirelessly using a Tesla coil. The Tesla loop had numerous useful applications, including remote telecommunication and early TV broadcasting. Vacuum tubes and solid-state transistors, on the other hand, eventually took their place as more advanced electrical transmission methods became available.

The traditional steam turbines, which were the predominant method of producing electrical power at the time, were not as efficient or dependable as the Tesla turbine, which was created to replace them. Tesla felt that a variety of energy sources, such as water, wind, and geothermal energy, could be harnessed to generate electricity utilising the Tesla turbine. Tesla's design for the Tesla Turbine is based on the principles of electromagnetic induction, which is the process of generating an electric current by moving a conductor through a magnetic field. The turbine consists of a rotor surrounded by a series of fixed electromagnetic coils, powered by an external electrical energy source. As the rotor rotates, it creates a magnetic field that interacts with the stationary coils, causing them to generate currents. This current is then fed into a generator, converting it into usable electricity.

There are numerous practical uses for the Tesla turbine in today's world. It is frequently utilized in industrial settings to generate electricity from nuclear power, renewable energy, fossil fuels, and other sources. It's also used to power electric vehicles and provide backup power for critical infrastructure, among other things. The Tesla turbine's high efficiency and dependability are key benefits. It can generate electricity from a wide variety of sources, including wind and geothermal energy, which are not always available or reliable. As a result, it is a crucial instrument for lowering our reliance on fossil fuels and raising the usage of renewable energy sources. It is still a crucial technology today, and new generations of engineers and inventors are continually motivated by its legacy.

Tesla revolutionized wireless power transfer with his efforts. In his idealised society, power lines would not be necessary for the wireless transfer of electricity, which would allow for its effective transmission across great distances. Although he did not live to see his vision of widespread wireless power transmission completely realised, his ground-breaking work paved the way for future advancements in wireless charging and power transfer technology.

However, these inventions represent just a fraction of Tesla's remarkable body of work. Generations of inventors, scientists, and engineers continue to be influenced and inspired by his concepts and technologies. The way we generate and distribute electricity interact with machines and envision the possibilities of technology have all been shaped by Tesla's unwavering belief in the power of his ideas and his unwavering pursuit of innovation.

A CLOSER LOOK AT MR. TESLA!

Several of Nikola Tesla's innovations went unnoticed, while others were lost when the fire burned his notes. His research was seized by the FBI at the end of his life, and it has just recently been made available to the general public. The Wardenclyffe Tower project stands as one of Nikola Tesla's most ambitious and captivating ventures. Conceived as a grand undertaking to transmit wireless power and revolutionize global communication, the project encountered numerous challenges and, ultimately, failed to achieve its intended objectives. The Wardenclyffe Tower is nevertheless a tribute to Tesla's bold concepts and his unwavering pursuit of ground-breaking breakthroughs despite its failure. The idea behind the Wardenclyffe Tower was to create a giant wireless transmission station capable of transmitting electrical energy and communication signals without the need for traditional wires or cables. Tesla envisioned a world where electricity could be harnessed and distributed wirelessly, providing seemingly limitless power to homes, businesses, and industries across vast distances. The tower, over 180 feet tall, will serve as the central hub for the wireless transmission system. To finance the project, Tesla sought financial support from a variety of sources, including Notable investors like JPMorgan. However, securing sufficient funding proved to be a daunting challenge. The size and scope of the project required considerable capital, and Tesla's unique ideas and uncertainty surrounding wireless power transmission made it difficult to secure the necessary financing.

Additionally, Tesla faced technical limitations and public scepticism. The idea of wireless electricity transmission was once met with scepticism and scepticism from the scientific community and the everyday public. Tesla's formidable claims and his popularity as an eccentric inventor from time to time hindered his capability to achieve substantial help and credibility. The lack of comprehensive understanding of his Wi-Fi energy transmission science similarly compounded the challenges he faced. Despite the challenges, Tesla pressed on with the undertaking and started construction of the Wardenclyffe Tower in Shoreham, Long Island, New York, in 1901. The tower's plan incorporated a massive underground structure, big electrical equipment, and a distinguished tower structure. However, as the building progressed, the lack of adequate funding grew to become a big hindrance. Tesla's non-stop need for extra monetary assistance strained his relationship with J.P. Morgan, and the investor's enthusiasm waned as he grew to be increasingly sceptical of the project's viability and profitability. The economic difficulties, mixed with Tesla's different ventures and criminal battles, compelled him to abandon the Wardenclyffe Tower project. As the property went into foreclosure in 1906, the tower and its machinery were eventually taken apart. The wireless power transmission system and world communication network that Tesla had envisioned never came to pass. Even though the Wardenclyffe Tower project's initial goals weren't met, its legacy and significance live on. The development of wireless communication, energy transfer, and the idea of a global network were all influenced by Tesla's vision for wireless power transmission, which anticipated technological improvements. The project served as a testament to Tesla's unwavering commitment to pushing the limits of innovation in the face of significant obstacles and setbacks. The Wardenclyffe site has undergone significant efforts to preserve and honour Tesla's legacy. The property was purchased and transformed into the Tesla Science Centre at Wardenclyffe, a museum and educational facility dedicated to celebrating Tesla's contributions to science and engineering.

The Tesla You Don'T Know

Although it's true that Tesla's innovations and achievements were substantial, they weren't always given the credit they deserved when he was alive. Nikola Tesla, being an enigmatic figure in history, has been surrounded by various controversies and misconceptions regarding his life and inventions. The brilliant inventor and visionary Nikola Tesla have frequently been cloaked in rumours and falsehoods that have persisted over time. Tesla made some amazing discoveries, but it's crucial to distinguish fact from fiction and dispel certain myths about his life and legacy.

One of the most famous controversies is the alleged rivalry between Tesla and Thomas Edison. It is often depicted as a battle between AC (Tesla) and DC (Edison) power systems, with Edison portrayed as the villain trying to discredit Tesla's work. While there have been differences in their business approaches and strategies, the extent of their personal rivalry is exaggerated in popular culture. Another misconception is that Tesla's Wardenclyffe Tower was intended to provide the world with free energy. While Tesla envisioned wireless power transmission, the tower itself was designed to demonstrate the feasibility of wireless communications and to serve as a business venture to transmit information and signals. It was not intended to provide unlimited free energy to the public. Tesla's work on directed energy weapons, often referred to as "death rays", has led to speculation and misunderstanding. Some believe that Tesla invented a powerful weapon capable of mass destruction. However, there is no concrete evidence to support this claim, and Tesla's actual intentions and progress on such a device remain unclear.

Tesla's eccentric conduct and unorthodox thoughts have led to speculation about his mental health. Some misconceptions propose that he used to be mentally unstable or suffered from prerequisites like obsessive-compulsive sickness (OCD) or autism. While Tesla did show off sure eccentricities, there is no conclusive evidence to aid these claims, and they frequently forget about his huge contributions to science and engineering. Numerous conspiracy theories endorse that Tesla's innovations were deliberately suppressed via powerful people or agencies due to their achievable disruptive nature. These theories frequently lack credible proof and fail to well know the complex factors that contribute to the success or failure of inventions. Some misconceptions attribute the innovations and discoveries of others to Tesla alone. While Tesla made outstanding contributions, he worked alongside and constructed upon the work of several scientists and engineers. It is important to renowned the collective efforts of the scientific community rather than attributing all achievements fully to Tesla. Tesla's life is now and again portrayed as one of unappreciated genius, with claims that he was not noted and his innovations stolen. While Tesla confronted challenges and did no longer usually get hold of the cognizance he deserved at some stage in his lifetime, he did get hold of acclaim and assistance from several individuals, which include incredible traders and scientists. The disputes and myths surrounding Nikola Tesla's life and achievements can be approached critically, and the historical context must be understood. Tesla made a lot of contributions, but it's important to distinguish fact from fiction and acknowledge how collaborative science is. We all have our own opinions and perspectives. Therefore, separating fact from fiction is crucial when examining the life and work of Nikola Tesla. While he was undoubtedly a brilliant inventor, it is important to sometimes avoid romanticizing or sensationalizing achievements. By critically evaluating historical records and credible sources, we can appreciate Tesla's true contributions and gain a more accurate understanding of his remarkable legacy.

SO MUCH MORE ABOUT TESLA...

The assumption that Nikola Tesla had many untold stories and facts surrounding his life and work is based on several factors. Tesla was considered a reserved person. He did not extensively document his private life, nor did he share details about his inventions and experiments. This reticence has contributed to a sense of intrigue and mystery surrounding his work. Compared to other inventors and scientists of his time, Tesla neither systematically kept meticulous records nor published his findings. Although he has authored numerous patents and scientific articles, there is a feeling that much of his work remains hidden or unexplored due to the limited documentation available. The mystery surrounding Tesla's life and work has been heightened by the dearth of thorough archives devoted to him. Over time, some of his personal documents and lab notes were misplaced or destroyed, creating gaps in our knowledge of his theories and experiments. There have been a lot of rumours, myths, and speculations about Tesla's alleged inventions, interactions with other famous people, and involvement with the government over the years. Even though these stories frequently lack evidence, they contribute to the aura of mystery surrounding Tesla. Occasionally, Tesla's ideas were considered revolutionary or ahead of their time. Consequently, during his lifetime, some of his ideas and theories were not fully understood. Because of this, there has been speculation about unexplored facets of his research as well as untold tales connected to his revolutionary concepts.

While Nikola Tesla conducted his experiments in Colorado Springs, his intense research did result in some unintended consequences. The nature of Tesla's work, which involved high-voltage and high-frequency electrical experiments, sometimes pushed the limits of the available electrical infrastructure and had unintended effects on the environment. Tesla used enormous amounts of electricity to generate extremely potent electromagnetic fields for his experiments at Colorado Springs. Tesla's experiments occasionally created a rapid increase in power consumption that was too much for the local power grid, resulting in brief blackouts in the neighbourhood. The electrical energy he was using was so great that it was beyond the capacity of the system at the time. One event, in particular, was the reported accidental electrocution of butterflies. Tesla's high-frequency electricity tests produced powerful electric fields close to his lab. It is reported that the electric discharges electrocuted butterflies that flew too close to the experiment. This unforeseen consequence draws attention to the potential environmental effects of strong electrical fields.

The Tesla You Don'T Know

It is true that after immigrating to the United States, Nikola Tesla had no permanent residence for most of his life. Instead, he frequently stayed in hotels in different cities, conducting his research and working on various projects. Tesla has faced financial challenges throughout his career and has struggled to maintain a stable income. This nomadic lifestyle allowed him the flexibility to continue his scientific pursuits without being tied to a specific location. While may have presented a challenge in terms of stability and personal comfort, it may also have given you the freedom to explore different avenues, collaborate with different people, and work on your inventions wherever the need arises.

It is frequently asserted that Nikola Tesla foresaw the idea of cell phones in 1926, demonstrating his astounding insight into wireless communication. Tesla discussed the possibilities of wireless technology and its effects on society in an interview that was published in Collier's magazine in 1926. He envisioned a future where individuals could carry small handheld devices that would allow them to communicate with one another wirelessly. Tesla described a device that resembled a "pocket instrument" or "pocket-size telephone", which he believed would enable people to connect instantly, regardless of their physical location. While Tesla's vision shared some similarities with the concept of cell phones, it is essential to recognize that his ideas were based on the principles of wireless telegraphy and his own experiments with the wireless transmission of signals. The actual development and realization of cell phones as we know them today involved the contributions of numerous inventors, engineers, and technological advancements over several decades. Building on earlier inventions like two-way radios and vehicle phones, the idea of mobile telephony, which eventually led to the development of mobile phones, started to take shape in the middle of the 20th century. Cell phones, portable handheld devices with cellular network connectivity, did not become generally accessible until the late 20th century. It is vital to distinguish between Tesla's philosophical discussions and the precise prediction of mobile phones as they exist today, even though his forward-thinking concepts and grasp of wireless communication were undoubtedly ahead of their time.

The strong propensity that Nikola Tesla had for cleanliness and hygiene was an intriguing aspect of his personality. When it came to keeping his surroundings clean, Tesla displayed traits of being a germaphobe and obsessive behaviours. White gloves were a Tesla trademark, especially when working with laboratory equipment or conducting experiments. He thought that this way of doing things helped keep things clean and prevent contamination. Tesla had a deep-seated need for cleanliness rituals and an obsession with cleanliness. Both his hygiene and the cleanliness of his workplace were very important to him. He was particular about the cleanliness of his lab equipment and frequently washed his hands multiple times. Tesla disliked germs and was concerned about diseases. He took great care to prevent infection and often sanitised his hands, tools, and surfaces. The widespread knowledge of diseases and the value of hygiene at the time may have contributed to his conduct as a germaphobe.

Tesla was also rumoured to dislike pearl jewellery because of the possibility of contamination. He thought that the tiny gaps in pearl jewellery would serve as a breeding ground for microbes. Tesla kept his workspace spotless and incredibly organised. He made a point of stressing orderliness since he thought it promoted productivity and clarity in his work. His meticulous approach was in direct conflict with disarray and mess. It should also be remembered that Tesla performed X-ray experiments and significantly advanced the field. Tesla's work on X-rays was more sophisticated than previously believed, according to recent studies. Compared to other scientists at the time, he was able to produce X-rays at frequencies that were greater.

THE ONE WHO LIT THE WORLD

Nikola's final days and passing were not met with the fanfare one might expect for such a remarkable mind. In New York City, Nikola Tesla died on January 7, 1943, at the age of 86. His scientific discoveries and inventions were hugely significant, but his later years were characterized by financial difficulties and a decline in public acclaim. Tesla died in relative obscurity, despite the significant contributions he made to modern society. During the later long stretches of his life, Tesla dwelled in different New York City lodgings. The New Yorker Hotel, where he lived for ten years, was one notable establishment. Tesla stayed in two hotel rooms on the 33rd floor, which were provided by the hotel. His final breath came from one of these rooms. The death of Tesla did not receive a lot of immediate attention. News of his death was overshadowed by the on-going events of World War II and media coverage was minimal. The loss of one of the greatest inventors of all time was largely unknown to the general public. Tesla's funeral was held on January 12, 1943, at the Cathedral of St. John the Divine in New York City. Despite the modest attendance, his funeral was attended by leaders in science and technology that paid tribute to the man whose inventions changed the world. Apart from this, the Tesla Company, officially known as Tesla, Inc., is an American electric vehicle and clean energy company founded in 2003 by entrepreneurs Martin Eberhard and Marc Tarpenning. Eberhard and Tarpenning named their company Tesla Motors, inspired by the brilliant Serbian-American inventor Nikola Tesla, who played a crucial role in the development of modern electrical systems. The name Tesla embodied the company's commitment to innovation and clean energy solutions.

Due to worries about possible military uses of Tesla's invention, the U.S. government took everything of his belongings after his passing, including his papers. In order to assess the significance of his study and guard against any secret material getting into the wrong hands, the FBI and other agencies conducted inquiries. Tesla's accomplishments have received renewed attention and admiration in the decades since his passing. His brilliance and forward-thinking concepts have won the attention of scientists, innovators, and fans around. His legacy has been recognised with numerous museums, statues, and dedications, ensuring that his influence on society will never be forgotten.

The Nikola Tesla Experience Centre has officially opened its doorways in the ancient town of Karlovac in Croatia. The centre is placed close to the Karlovac Grammar School building, which the famous inventor attended and graduated from 150 years ago. The centre guarantees to take visitors on an immersive experience through the life and accomplishments of one of the world's greatest inventors, Nikola Tesla. The middle combines a museum, innovation, entrepreneurship, and tourism, supplying younger people with an attractive possibility to acquire information about Tesla. The core covers nearly 800 rectangular meters and facets of interactive exhibits, multimedia presentations, and a 3D hologram of Tesla. The centre also has a present keep where site visitors can buy Tesla-themed souvenirs. The opening ceremony was once attended by the Prime Minister of the Republic of Croatia, Andrej Plenković, and the Minister of Culture, Nina Obuljen Korzinek. The core is expected to entice traffic from around the world and will be a principal tourist appeal in Karlovac.

The centre offers state-of-the-art exhibitions, interactive exhibits, and engaging multimedia presentations. Visitors can see Tesla's 3D hologram, which is one of the highlights of the centre. The centre also houses exhibits showcasing Tesla's revolutionary inventions, including the Tesla coil, the rotating magnetic field, and the AC motor. Afterward, visitors can enjoy multimedia presentations on Tesla's visionary concepts and the impact of his work on modern technology. The centre also looks at Tesla's personal life, including his love of poetry, music, and food, as well as his bacteriophobia and attachment to a certain pigeon. There is a gift shop downtown where visitors can purchase Tesla-themed memorabilia. The centre includes a classroom and an amphitheatre where visitors can enjoy lectures and presentations about Tesla's life and work. Finally, the downtown café offers visitors the opportunity to order drinks in a futuristic way. Well, I believe that anyone interested in Nikola Tesla's life and work should pay a visit to the Nikola Tesla Experience Centre in Karlovac. The centre's exhibits and displays offer a comprehensive and captivating look at Tesla's ground-breaking discoveries, avant-garde ideas, and private life. The facility will be a significant tourist destination in Karlovac and is anticipated to draw tourists from all over the world.

Several writers and researchers have been fascinated by Nikola Tesla's life and work, which has resulted in the release of many books that explore different facets of his life, inventions, and contributions to science. These works provide analysis, biographical information, and in-depth analyses of Tesla's concepts and their effects. One of the most thorough biographies of Tesla's life, "Tesla: Man out of Time" by Margaret Cheney examines his early years, his career in Europe and America, as well as his various inventions and experiments.

It explores Tesla's oddities, his imaginative concepts, and the difficulties he encountered throughout his career. Similarly, "Wizard: The Life and Times of Nikola Tesla" by Marc Seifer offers a detailed examination of Tesla's life. While "Tesla: Inventor of the Electrical Age" by W. Bernard Carlson combines biographical details with a focus on Tesla's inventions and their impact on modern society.

It examines Tesla's new-fangled work in wireless energy transmission, wireless communication, and alternating current (AC) systems. Additionally, it delves into the difficulties Tesla encountered in promoting his ideas and obtaining financial backing. Whereas, "My Inventions: The Autobiography of Nikola Tesla" is a collection of Tesla's own writings that provides valuable insights into his thoughts, experiences, and inventions. Collectively, these works ensure that Tesla's remarkable contributions to science and technology will be remembered and cherished for generations to come.

However, the genius of Nikola Tesla can be attributed to his visionary outlook, in-depth comprehension of the fundamentals of electrical engineering, prolific inventiveness, unconventional thinking, and dedication to science, forward-looking perspective, and multidisciplinary approach.

His remarkable contributions have had a lasting impact on the world, influencing how electricity is harnessed and used and influencing technological advancements that still have an impact on our lives today. Generations of scientists, inventors, and innovators continue to be inspired by Tesla's genius to push the boundaries of human knowledge and imagination.

Printed in Great Britain
by Amazon